THE AMAZING PHOTOGRAPHY OF **IGOR SIWANOWICZ**

# MONSTERS AMONG US

LEVEL **2** READER

READING LEVEL
GRADES 1 TO 3

Photography © Igor Siwanowicz
Text © Dalmatian Press, LLC.

Written by Kathryn Knight

Published by Dalmatian Press, LLC. All rights reserved.
Printed in Guangzhou, Guangdong, China.
Franklin, Tennessee 37068-2068. 1-866-418-2572.
No part of this book may be reproduced or copied in any form without written permission
from the copyright owner. CE14268/0711

There is beauty all around us. Look closely as you wander through your yard. You may also see...

the monsters among us!

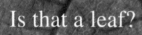

Is that a leaf?

...or something chewing?

Is that a twig with thorns?

…or a terror with horns?

There are eyes that watch

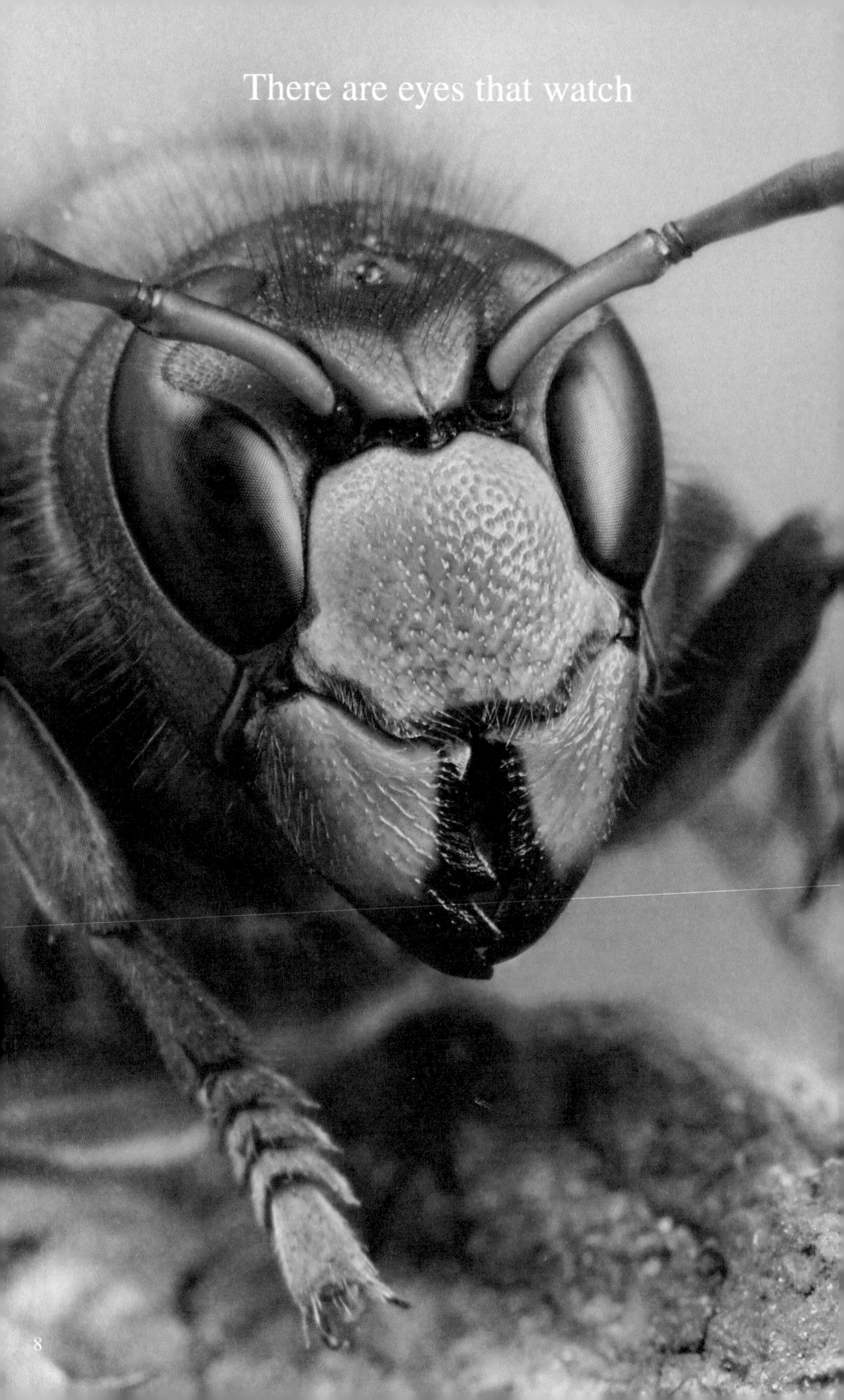

and jaws that snap!

Clicking, clasping claws that trap!

They're odd
and eerie…

...hairy and scary.

Lurking by day.

Stalking by night.

What a fright!

They may talk about you.

Does that make you uneasy?

Do red eyes and goblins with snouts
make you queasy?

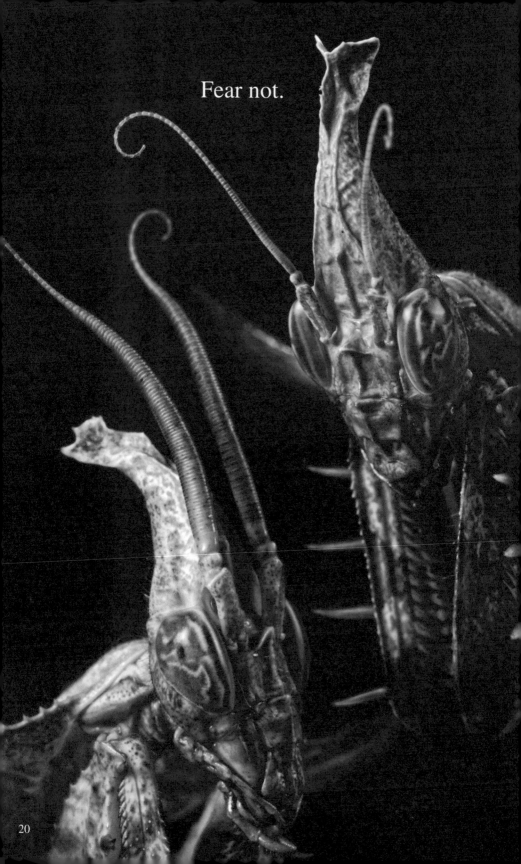

Fear not.

Even though
creepy monsters
completely
surround us—

—confound us!

—astound us!

—they're simply
a part of…

# ...the beauty around us.

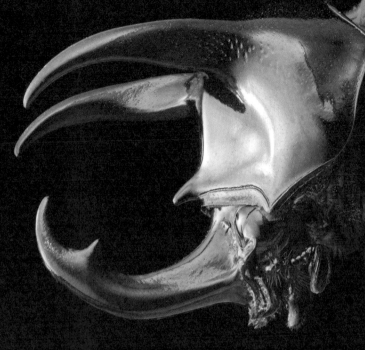